Byja Blueprint

An Introductory
Guide to
Direct Primary Care

For Doctors, Patients,
and Businesses

Byron Jasper, MD, MPH

ISBN: 979-8-991-24261-5 (paperback)
ISBN: 979-8-991-24260-8 (eBook)

Printed books may be purchased in bulk for promotional, educational, or business use. Please contact us via email at byjainfo@byja.org for more details and further assistance.

First Edition: August 2024

A quick word of thanks...

I am incredibly grateful for your interest in this book and for taking the time to explore the world of Direct Primary Care (DPC). Your decision to journey through these pages reflects a shared commitment to enhancing the quality of healthcare for yourself, your family, or your business. I truly hope that this book provides the valuable insights and practical guidance that you are seeking, whether you are a patient, healthcare professional, or business leader.

For more information about our Direct Primary Care practice, Byja Clinic, and how we can serve your healthcare needs, please visit our website at **www.byja.org**.

Additionally, if you are interested in learning about and supporting our nonprofit organization, Byja Charitable Alliance, which aims to make DPC accessible to underserved communities, please visit **www.byjaca.org**.

Your continued support and engagement are invaluable to us and I truly appreciate it.

Warm regards,

Dr. Byron Jasper

Table Of Contents

Aim and Objectives

Healthcare is on the brink of a transformative change, and leading this change is the Direct Primary Care (DPC) model. DPC promises to redefine our approach to personal wellness and medical care as a whole. This innovative framework is rapidly gaining traction, celebrated for its remarkable cost-efficiency, its streamlined operations, and above all, its unparalleled ability to deliver superior patient care. DPC stands as a catalyst for freedom in an industry often shackled by the constraints of traditional insurance-based systems. It promises patients the liberty to choose a physician who truly listens, dedicating ample time to each consultation. It empowers physicians to prioritize meaningful patient interactions over the endless sea of paperwork. And it provides both employers and employees with a path to significantly reduce their healthcare expenses by investing in what's genuinely necessary, rather than succumbing to the mandates of large insurance entities.

This book looks deep into the essence of Direct Primary Care, sharing information about its growth, celebrating its rising status as a compelling alternative to the traditional fee-for-service model, and unveiling its role as the preferred solution for the healthcare dilemmas facing patients, doctors, and businesses. As we journey through the intricacies of DPC, we'll confront and clarify the common questions and misconceptions that cloud its understanding, illuminating the path to truth about the model. Our mission is to equip you with the insight needed to see why Direct Primary Care shines as the best choice for your health, your family's well-being, and your business's healthcare strategy. Through this writing, our aim extends beyond mere education; we seek to inspire, leading you toward a future where healthcare transcends expectation, becoming deeply personal and exceptionally effective.

Foreword

Imagine a world where your healthcare isn't dictated by insurance companies or burdened by endless paperwork. Picture a system where your doctor knows you personally, understands your health history, and has the time to provide the care you truly need. This is the world of Direct Primary Care, a life-changing model of healthcare that Dr. Byron Jasper has passionately embraced and now eloquently promotes in this book.

My name is Markeiya Polite Jasper. I'm a board-certified OB/GYN, and the aforementioned Dr. Jasper is my husband. As someone who practices in the traditional medical system, I greatly admire the DPC model and truly value the impact that it's had on Byron and so many doctors like him. And after joining him at several recent DPC conferences across the country, I also see the beneficial effects that this model can have on the future of medical care overall.

When he first introduced me to the Direct Primary Care concept, I was struck by its simplicity and effectiveness. It was, and remains, a model that brings medicine back to its roots, focusing on the direct relationship between doctor and patient. This model is free from the complexities and constraints seen within insurance-based systems and it is regularly celebrated for its remarkable cost-efficiency, streamlined operations, and unparalleled ability to deliver superior patient care.

As someone who has observed Byron's evolution in healthcare throughout this journey, I've witnessed firsthand the profound benefits DPC can have on physicians, patients, and businesses. If you're an employer who is curious as to how cutting out the middleman could lead to better health outcomes, I know you'll find this book enlightening. I also know if you're a primary care doctor who feels burned out by the current system, you will read this book and discover a system of primary care that can reignite a passion for your calling.

Specialty physicians such as myself will also find value in this book, as it demonstrates how DPC offers a way to optimize patient care, especially for those with extensive co-morbidities requiring extended time and attention. And for those patients who are comparing Direct Primary Care with existing traditional healthcare models, the detailed comparisons found in this book will provide you with valuable insights and examples as to how DPC wins this match up, over and over again.

Simply said, this book is a must-read for anyone interested in the revolution happening in primary care as a result of DPC. Readers will learn how Direct Primary Care saves significant time, energy, and money for both individuals and businesses. They will also be reminded of all the inefficiencies and frustrations of conventional primary care setups, and continually see how

10

DPC prioritizes an essential, but often neglected, principle in medicine – the doctor-patient relationship must remain the preeminent focus in order to properly deliver the highest quality of patient care.

Byron's dedication to this cause is evident in every chapter, and his expertise shines through as he makes a compelling case for why DPC is the future of healthcare. So, I encourage you to turn the page and prepare to be informed and inspired. You're about to take a journey that will fundamentally change the way you view healthcare in its entirety, just as it did for me.

With best wishes,

Dr. Markeiya Polite Jasper

Introduction

If you're diving into this guide, chances are you're on a quest for a richer, more fulfilling approach to healthcare – whether you're seeking care, providing it, or offering it to your team. Maybe you've stumbled upon this narrative in your search for alternatives, or perhaps a colleague or friend pointed you in this direction. Whatever the initial reasoning may be, it's likely that the conventional, insurance-driven healthcare model hasn't quite hit the mark for you, and it's failing to deliver the depth of care, attention, and value you, your patients, or your employees truly deserve. And I'm willing to bet you've heard about something called Direct Primary Care (or DPC) and, although you may not be entirely familiar with the ins and outs of it, the promise it holds for transforming healthcare has piqued your interest.

Well, you're in good company on this journey. When I first ventured down this path, I was in search of a healthcare model that didn't just pay lip service to better care but actually delivered on its promises – enhancing patient experiences, improving health outcomes, and doing so in a way that made financial sense for everyone involved. This guide is the fruit of that exploration. Here, I aim to demystify Direct Primary Care, examining its significant advantages over traditional models, tackling the myths around it, and sharing stories of its profound impact on both doctors and their patients.

The Triple Aim of healthcare – to improve the patient experience of care, improve the health of populations, and reduce per capita costs of healthcare – resonates deeply with DPC's core values. This viewpoint has revolutionized my perspective as to what healthcare can and should be. By fostering direct, meaningful connections between patients and their doctors, cutting through the unnecessary bureaucratic red tape, and prioritizing healthcare decisions that align with our shared values, DPC sets a new standard for healthcare expectations.

For me, embracing Direct Primary Care wasn't just a choice, it was a revelation. It showed me how healthcare could focus on cultivating the doctor-patient relationship, emphasizing quality at every turn. By removing the barriers that traditional healthcare systems often erect, DPC allows for a healthcare experience that is not only more affordable and accessible, but also of superior quality.

As we navigate through this guide together, my hope is that it serves as more than an introduction to Direct Primary Care. I want it to be your roadmap to empowered, personalized, and inclusive care within a model that places health and well-being at its heart. Let's explore how DPC is not only meeting but exceeding the Triple Aim of healthcare, redefining what it means to deliver patient-centered care in today's medical landscape.

Chapter 1
A Brief Look at
What Is Wrong With the
Traditional Primary Care Model
for Patients

All right, let's have a real chat about what's going on in the world of traditional primary care. So, you've probably been there – sitting in a waiting room that feels more like a holding pen, thumbing through a magazine from 2012, wondering if the receptionist has forgotten you were there. Sound familiar? It's one of those universal experiences we've all shared, but honestly, it's just the opening act in the traditional primary care circus.

Now, picture this: You're excited about dining at this restaurant your best friend and favorite sibling have raved about. You call ahead, make a reservation months in advance because, well, that's the only way to ensure you get a table.

Fast forward to the big night. You show up fifteen minutes early to the restaurant just like the hostess recommended when you made your reservation months ago, and what do you find? A packed lobby and that very same hostess telling you to have a seat and wait until they call your name.

You're thinking, "No biggie. I'm early and I've got a reservation that was made months ago." But as the minutes turn into an hour then an hour and a half, you're left wondering if they've started growing the protein and veggies for your meal out back. Finally, your name is called, and they usher you to your table! And just as you're settling in, ready to savor this experience and enjoy the meal you've anticipated for so long, the waiter's rushing you. It's like your food is coming at you on a conveyor belt – appetizers, salad, main course, and dessert – all flying at you. Before you know it, you're being handed your coat and your keys, then gently nudged out the door because the next twenty people with reservations are tapping their feet in the waiting area, likely to have the same "amazing" experience.

Now, imagine if every dining experience was like this. You'd likely never go back to those restaurants and might even swear off eating out altogether, right? In any other industry, this model would tank faster than you can say, "Check, please!" Yet, it's a standard practice in traditional primary care, leaving patients feeling just as rushed and undervalued as our hypothetical diners.

Isn't it wild how you can book an appointment months in advance in our traditional primary care model and still end up counting the ceiling tiles in the waiting room? So you have no choice but to settle into the least uncomfortable chair in the doctor's waiting room for what feels like an eternity. And let's not add the idea of you not feeling well to this scenario of endless waiting. We all know you could have binge-watched your favorite series or mastered a new recipe in the time it takes just to move from the waiting room to the exam room. It's a universal truth: the average wait time feels less like a brief pause and more like a time warp, where minutes stretch into hours and your patience is tested to its limits. Which brings me to my next point...

When you are finally called back to the exam room, it feels like a sprint through the actual visit. Ever felt like your doctor's visits are on a stopwatch? It's like, the moment you sit down, the clock starts ticking, and you're lucky if you can get a word in edgewise about what's actually bothering you. Our physicians are juggling so many patients that both doctors and patients end up getting short-changed on the one thing that matters most – *time.*

This whirlwind of brief visits isn't just frustrating, it's a domino effect. You end up needing more follow-ups for things you couldn't cover the first time. You also know that these low quality, brief, and frequent follow-up visits lead to you having poor health outcomes and further drive your healthcare costs upward, since each visit results in new medical expenses. And those same visits just pack the doctor's schedule even tighter in the future. It's a vicious cycle of long waits, rushed chats, higher bills, and feeling like you're just another item on the day's to-do list.

Accessibility is another headache especially if you're living in a rural area or can't easily get around. Just getting to an appointment can feel like planning a moon landing simply because the traditional model isn't exactly known for bending over backward to fit your schedule. So, if you're trying to get that close follow-up appointment to discuss things that you couldn't review in your most recent rushed visit – expect to mark your calendar weeks, if not months, out.

And have you noticed how one-size-fits-all your visits can feel? Take more pills. Order more expensive tests. See more specialists. It's as if there's a standard script, and everyone's just playing their part. But you're unique, right? Your care should be tailored to you, not just some general guideline.

Don't even get me started on insurance. Navigating what's covered, what's not, and why it feels like you need a special translator just to understand your medical bill – it's enough to make your head spin. And oftentimes, it feels like you're making decisions based on what your wallet can handle, not what's best for your health, mostly because there is no true price transparency with just about everything.

There's also this whole vibe of playing defense with your health – dealing with problems as they pop up rather than working together to prevent them. It's like we're always a step behind, trying to catch up, instead of staying ahead of the game.

It all underscores the urgency for change and the appeal of models like Direct Primary Care. Here, the focus is on quality, individualized attention, transparency, and cutting out the wait –

essentially, ensuring every "diner" feels like they're getting their personal chef's special treatment, every time.

Chapter 2
A Brief Look at
What Is Wrong With the
Traditional Primary Care Model
for Doctors

Let's flip the script for a moment and look at traditional primary care from the other side of the exam table – the physicians' side. You know those go-to doctors when you're not feeling your best who are supposed to be your health heroes; scratch that... let's go with the MVPs in your team's journey to the championship level of wellness. But here's the twist: in the classic healthcare setup, these dedicated doctors often end up becoming adversaries to your health or seeming to be on the other team, stifling you from becoming victorious in your health journey.

Those same physicians, who likely became a doctor to care for patients because of a calling to help the sick and indigent no matter their circumstance, are juggling an astonishing twenty-five to fifty patients daily with each patient interaction becoming its own fleeting moment. They may have a visit on their schedule every fifteen to twenty minutes if they're lucky – but in reality they squeeze in a visit every seven to ten minutes. That's barely enough time to scratch the surface of what's bothering you, much less to forge any meaningful bond.

I must say it again: this whirlwind of quick visits creates a frustrating domino effect. Yet, it's not just for patients; it is for both parties. We already mentioned that the patients are often left with unresolved issues, necessitating more follow-up appointments and how this just crams more into the doctor's already overflowing schedule.

But the story doesn't end when the clinic's doors lock for the night. That's when Round Two begins for the doctors. Picture them, settled in for the evening, not to relax, but to tackle the mountain of clinical notes for every patient seen that day and the day before that and the day before that. This charting marathon isn't just a chore; it's a time-consuming beast that devours their evenings and erodes the precious downtime they have away from the clinic. The complexity of these notes, especially for those patients with intricate health needs, means less and less time for personal rest for the doctors and them regularly missing out on important family moments.

And just in case you thought this charting at home was the only thing the doctors have to do when they are not seeing patients, let's not forget the avalanche of medication refills, lab reviews, specialist referrals, and patient callbacks piling up for them. Ahhh, a never-ending to-do list that demands attention amid an already hectic day. I'm sure if you asked them, they would confirm that it's exactly why they went to medical school – to have their success in this traditional model ironically measured by the volume of patient visits they can see rather than the quality of care they deliver.

The Hidden Battle

Let's peel back another layer of the traditional primary care saga and spotlight a less talked about but deeply impactful aspect. This relentless pace is more than just exhausting; it's a breeding ground for what's known as moral injury. It's the pain that comes from knowing what care your patients need, but being trapped in a system that forces you to choose between the most ideal care and what the day's schedule allows. I know it well and dealt with it regularly while caring for many of our underserved and underinsured patients in the traditional fee-for-service model. Every rushed visit and unaddressed concern isn't just a logistical issue; it's a blow to the very reason most of us physicians donned white coats in the first place – to care deeply and thoroughly for our patients regardless of their insurance coverage.

Adding Salt to the Moral Injury Wound

Imagine navigating a healthcare journey where the map is drawn not by the needs of the traveler but by a third party, whose primary language seems to be red tape and fine print. This is the reality for many physicians dealing with the traditional, insurance-based model of care, a reality that compounds the moral injury they face daily. Doctors trained to make the best decisions for their patients' health find themselves having to navigate a maze of approvals and denials. It's a scenario where a treatment plan that should take minutes to decide becomes a drawn-out negotiation, not with the disease, but with paperwork and policies. The administrative burdens placed on physicians by insurance companies are not just about paperwork; they're about the hours of labor that go into justifying medical decisions, chasing prior-authorizations, and appealing denied claims.

Each of these tasks pulls doctors away from the clinical work they are passionate about and trained for over the course of seven or more years. They entered medicine, studied diligently throughout medical school, and worked tirelessly within and beyond their residency programs to treat patients – not to navigate an administrative labyrinth. This constant tug-of-war between providing care and meeting insurance requirements often leaves physicians feeling like they're failing their patients, despite their best efforts. This dynamic can deeply frustrate physicians, as it directly conflicts with their primary commitment to patient care, forcing them into choices that align more with policy than with medical best practices.

The involvement of insurance companies in medical decision-making doesn't just strain physicians; it also impacts the quality and timeliness of care that patients receive. The wait for insurance approvals often delays necessary treatments, forcing doctors to watch their patients suffer needlessly and undergo a sense of helplessness to act swiftly and in the best interest of their patients' health. It's a reminder that their ability to practice medicine as they see fit is often compromised, leaving them to question whether they can truly fulfill their oath to do no harm.

All of these challenges are a glaring reflection of a system that's overtly broken, leading to doctor dissatisfaction, escalating healthcare costs, and far less-than-ideal health outcomes for patients. The crisis in primary care is real, marked by overworked doctors, burnout, and a looming shortage of PCPs, which only exacerbates the situation.

So you may be wondering, with such a broken system, why does anyone stick around? The truth is, many don't realize there's a much better alternative. Enter Direct Primary Care – a model of hope that directly addresses these pain points and reimagines what primary care should look like.

In our next chapter, we'll take a closer look at DPC, a model where healthcare regains its humanity, where doctor-patient connections are nurtured, not rushed, and where outstanding care and transparency is the norm, not the exception. We'll also see how it not only promises but delivers a way for physicians to practice medicine that aligns with the ideals that draw many to the field, offering a reprieve from the insurance-driven dilemmas that have long plagued the healthcare environment. So, stick with us. The dive into DPC might just be the refreshing perspective you've been seeking, offering a viable and compassionate alternative to the traditional primary care grind.

Chapter 3
Fundamentals of
Direct Primary Care

All right, enough with all of the negatives that exist within the traditional system as we know it. I would rather be positive and find a more uplifting viewpoint for this situation. To do this, we should look no further than what Direct Primary Care is all about and as we look closer, I'm sure you will agree it's like tossing out the old, clunky playbook of healthcare and trying something that, frankly, makes a lot more sense. So, relax and take a deep breath. I know DPC will be a game-changer for you in the way you ultimately look at the healthcare scene as it brings a much needed change of pace and puts the focus right back where it belongs: on you and your doctor.

To keep it simple, I'll begin by saying that DPC is like this breath of fresh air in the healthcare world. Why, you ask? Imagine having this direct line to your physician, where you're not jumping through insurance hoops just to get the care you need. That's right, no insurance companies calling the shots on your care dictating how long you get to chat with your doctor or how quick your visit should be when you're sick. Instead, it's based on a pretty straightforward concept that you likely are already using in other areas of your day-to-day life.

In Direct Primary Care, you pay an inexpensive monthly fee directly to your doctor's clinic much like how you pay a set subscription to your favorite streaming service or for your gym membership. But this subscription is for something a tad more vital: your health. This fee covers a whole suite of primary care services, which we will discuss in more detail in a moment, without surprise fees. And the best part? There are no insurance companies in the mix. It's just you and your doctor, making health decisions without a third party muddying the waters.

Now, you might be wondering, *Why should I avoid using my insurance for regular primary care visits?* I'm glad you asked. It's all about cutting out the middleman to make things smoother and more personal. DPC doctors get to spend quality time with you because they're not playing by the insurance companies' rulebook, which often feels like it's more about checking boxes than checking up on your health. Plus, without the hassle of filing insurance claims, everyone's life gets a bit easier—less paperwork, lower costs, and no surprise bills. It's a win-win.

You should know by a few of my previous references that I love analogies and use them quite often with my patients. So allow me to further clarify how the DPC concept works with an analogy that really drives it home. Think about your car insurance. You've got it, but you're not using it for everyday maintenance like fueling up, tire repairs, or oil changes, right? You wouldn't drive to a gas station or mechanic shop and ask them if they are in your network. That's because it's there for the big stuff like accidents and major repairs. Now, apply that same logic to health insurance. Imagine keeping it in your back pocket for the big, unexpected health issues, while your DPC membership handles the day-to-day healthcare needs. Makes sense, doesn't it? It's about using insurance wisely, which would actually help bring down healthcare related costs across the board.

With DPC, doctors are also benefiting as they are finally figuring out how to step off the traditional healthcare hamster wheel. DPC doctors are seeing fewer patients each day, which means they're not bogged down with endless charting after hours. This translates to more face-to-face time with you during visits, less time wasted in the waiting room, and a healthcare experience that feels, well, more human. And the membership fee? It's uncomplicated, inexpensive, and transparent— set by the doctor and shared with you right upfront, so you're not left guessing about costs.

Byja Blueprint

But wait, there's more and it continues to get better. I mentioned no surprise fees earlier, but here's a kicker—there's also no co-pays and no deductibles in the DPC model. That's right, healthcare without the hidden fees. Much like being able to enjoy a meal without worrying about the final bill at the end because you knew all the menu prices in the beginning.

Now, when we stack DPC against traditional primary care, or even concierge medicine, the differences start to really pop. With DPC, it's not about exclusivity or hefty price tags that are a huge secret; it's about accessibility, transparency, and genuinely putting the patient first. It's a model that feels more like a partnership than a transaction, and that's an amazing concept. So, what do you think? Sounds a bit more appealing than the usual runaround with insurance for every sneeze, bump, bruise, aching, or check-up, right? Well keep reading, and we'll dive deeper into how DPC is shaking up the healthcare system in all the right ways. It's a journey worth taking, especially if you're like the majority of people in the traditional model and you're tired of the same old healthcare headaches.

Chapter 4
The Amazing Benefits of
Direct Primary Care for Patients

You know, there's this saying that floats around in the direct primary care universe: *"If you've seen one DPC practice, you've seen one DPC practice."* Pretty simple, but it really hits the nail on the head. Every DPC clinic is its own unique practice, with its own culture, membership pricing, and menu of clinical services. We're going to deeply explore that variety soon, but first, let's chat about what ties all these diverse practices together. Despite their individual flair, there's an array of amazing features that most DPC practices have in common, creating this awesome shared identity within the DPC space.

Common DPC Concepts

First up, let's talk about options in primary care. Have you ever had the chance to meet your doctor *before* you scheduled an appointment with them? Or pick a physician outside your insurance network *without* worrying about costs? Odds are, both answers were no. It's strange, right? We get to meet our lawyers, barbers, or hairstylists first to ensure they're the right fit for us. But when it comes to choices like this in the traditional model, our hands are tied. You're usually stuck choosing doctors based on who accepts your insurance, not necessarily who has a similar background or shares similar beliefs or who takes the most time to listen to your concerns.

Better yet, how about who's the best fit for you and your health needs? This system that lacks true choice often leads to patients skipping essential primary care, resulting in worse health outcomes, unnecessary emergency room visits, and soaring healthcare costs.

Now, enter the world of Direct Primary Care. This model breaks the choiceless cycle, letting you choose your doctor without the insertion of an insurance middleman. Whether you're insured or not, DPC gives you the freedom to pick a physician who aligns with your needs, beliefs, and budget, enhancing your health outcomes without the extra financial strain.

Now, onto the topic everyone is curious about when it comes to Direct Primary Care: pricing. This is a multilayered topic within DPC, but when it's truly understood one can easily see the savings continually add up. We will begin by looking at the membership side of things.

With Direct Primary Care, you're not playing a guessing game with medical bills related to your visits. The monthly membership fee covers just about all of your primary care needs which includes unlimited in person clinical visits as well as unlimited telemedicine visits.

Go back to our streaming analogy from earlier. When you stream, you don't pay by the show, song, or movie. Instead you pay a flat fee each month and it's unlimited usage from there.

Same goes for most DPC memberships. They are usually charged as a single, upfront monthly membership fee in exchange for clinical services delivered by the doctor. Oh, and just a heads up, some DPC clinics will even throw in a deal that when you pay for your membership quarterly or annually, they'll toss in some cool perks or discounts for going that route. So you can kiss all of those surprise copays and baffling deductibles goodbye with Direct Primary Care.

You should know that membership costs for DPC practices vary by location but are designed to be affordable and transparent. We say transparent because many DPC clinics across the country proudly post their monthly membership prices online on their official websites and social media accounts. The key word here is proudly, because we know many traditional primary care practices cannot do this – mostly because they don't know how much things cost because of the enigma of insurance plans they have to deal with on a daily basis.

The other idea is they simply *won't* do this as a strategic choice because keeping their pricing a mystery to patients allows them to charge exorbitant prices without too many eyebrows being raised. So, unlike the usual primary care maze, where figuring out costs feels like solving a mystery thanks to the endless puzzle of insurance plans, DPC clinics routinely and repeatedly cut through the confusion.

Going back to the part about DPC being budget-friendly, the average monthly membership fee ranges from $75 to $125 for adults. This equates to about $2.50 to $4.17 per day to have access to your physician when you need it most. That's probably less than a fancy coffee or a value meal at a fast food spot, and it's for something far more priceless. Membership fees are typically lower for pediatric patients in DPC practices with some clinics even decreasing the price per child for families with more children. This often equates to large savings, both in time and money, for larger families. And because DPC practices aren't tangled up in all of the insurance bureaucracy, they can pass those savings right back to you. So, you'll often hear me say that DPC is great for both your physical and financial health.

DPC membership fees cover a wide range of primary care services beyond unlimited clinic visits and we will dig into those services in a moment. But before we do that let's first look at a direct comparison that further demonstrates how DPC outshines the traditional model.

We'll start with the sizes of their respective patient panels. In a Direct Primary Care setting, a physician typically manages a patient panel of around 500 to 650 patients. This is significantly less than the 2,000 to 3,000 patients often seen in traditional models. This smaller patient load allows for more personalized care, with DPC doctors having no more than 10 patient visits per day in comparison to traditional doctors who usually have somewhere between 24 to 60 visits per day. Considering the number of visits per day we just referenced, it's easy to see that DPC visits often range from 30 to 60 minutes per visit in contrast to the 10 to 15 minutes often allocated in traditional settings.

To drive this point home, DPC doctors actually spend the full 30 minutes or 60 minutes of each visit with their patients. Those traditional doctors spend between 7 to 10 minutes with their patients, even though those patients are scheduled for visits with longer timeframes. So instead of rushing through patient visits to meet quotas or insurance requirements, DPC doctors actually spend quality time with each patient, addressing their questions and concerns openly and comprehensively.

Now you may think I'm just making up the idea that traditional doctors only spend 7 to 10 minutes with their patients. I would respond to that by saying something I learned growing up and going to church in the South. *"If you can't say 'Amen,' say 'ouch'!"* This translates into three simple words...the truth hurts. Yet, I'll clarify how this 7 to 10 minutes of time spent is more than mere hearsay.

So, in the traditional model, most doctors average between 24 to 60 patients per full clinic day. You can think of this as 12 patients in the morning and 12 patients in the afternoon, for a total of 24 patients in one day or 30 patients in the morning and 30 patients in the afternoon for a total of 60 patients in a full day. In this model, each patient is scheduled for a 15 or 20 minute clinic visit with the doctor during the course of that doctor's clinic sessions. Considering those numbers, if we are at the lower side of patient volume that was just mentioned this boils down to about 3 or 4 patients per hour in an 8-hour work day which is approximately 24 to 32 patients per day (e.g., 3 patients per hour x 8 hours = 24 patients per day, or 4 patients per hour x 8 hours = 32 patients per day). If we are at the higher end of the patient volume (60 patients per clinic day) patients are still scheduled for 15 or 20 minute clinic visits with the doctor. [Thank you, insurance companies.] But when you realistically review that approach to scheduling, the math breaks down to about 7 to 8 minutes per visit with the doctor (e.g., 7.5 patients per hour x 8 hours = 60 patients per day). This means that each patient in this clinic will only have 8 minutes with the doctor within that hour of clinic time.

The traditional model gives you rushed, glance-at-your-watch-every-two-seconds kind of visits. But the visits that provide real, quality time with your doctor to build a rapport and fully address each of your health concerns is a staple of Direct Primary Care. In the DPC world, the clock isn't the boss – your health is. Our appointments in

DPC feel less like a speed dating round and more like a relaxed get together with a friend who genuinely cares about your well-being. These extended visits allow your doctor to really listen to your concerns, peel back each of the layers of your health questions, and work with you to craft individualized care plans. It's the kind of thorough, attentive care that makes you feel seen and valued – not just another appointment on the schedule. I'm proud to add that my longest DPC appointment with a patient was right around 2 ½ hours and it was exactly what that patient needed at that moment.

Now, let's move on to a favorite part for most Direct Primary Care patients – direct access to your physician. We have said quite a few times already that DPC is built on the premise that healthcare should be uncomplicated, personal, and accessible. Imagine having your doctor's cell number and being able to call, text, or email them just when you need it most, whether it's during business hours, after business hours, late at night, and even on weekends. Well you can quit imagining this is a thing and come to the realization that's DPC for you!

In DPC practices, this kind of direct access isn't an add-on; it's part of the base package of services and your monthly membership fee covers it all. So, there are no extra charges for every call, every message, or any email you send. By doing this DPC breaks down one of the biggest barriers to receiving high quality healthcare – speaking to your physician when it's actually convenient for you. Our patients have actually said that DPC feels more like they have a trusted doctor in their family rather than a distant, formal relationship defined by excessive appointments and packed waiting rooms.

Speaking of packed waiting rooms, this brings us our next two benefits of DPC: ease of scheduling appointments and no waiting during those appointments. We all know navigating the traditional healthcare model to schedule an appointment can often feel like an uphill battle, loaded with frustration and uncertainty. Imagine feeling under the weather or dealing with a sudden injury, and the first hurdle you encounter is trying to secure an appointment with your primary care physician. In the conventional setup, patients can find themselves stuck in a seemingly endless loop of waiting, often spanning anywhere from weeks to months, just to complete a scheduled visit. This dreary anticipation is not just about marking calendars and counting days; it's about the unsettling realization that urgent care or emergency room visits become the reluctant go-to for issues your primary care doctor could have addressed, had they simply been more reachable.

So, why does the DPC model emerge as a ray of hope in this context? Imagine the relief and convenience of being able to schedule same-day or next-day appointments with just a simple phone call or text. This model not only sidesteps the dreaded wait times associated with traditional healthcare but also dispels the anxiety and second-guessing about whether seeking medical attention is "worth it." The traditional model's convoluted exercise of attempting to get someone on the phone then confirming an appointment at a convenient time with the same physician and all at an unambiguous cost often feels exhaustive for those navigating the process. This inevitably leads many to postpone or entirely ignore medical issues, a decision that can have dire consequences.

The irony in the traditional model is stark when it comes to handling sick patients. The all-too-familiar scene of a waiting room crowded with individuals, each battling their ailments, is a breeding ground for discomfort and, ironically, more illness. Seriously, who decided it made sense to corral a variety of sick individuals together, only to leave them waiting indefinitely for care? No one seems to know, yet it's so very commonplace in healthcare.

Well, DPC clinics break away from this norm, virtually eliminating the waiting room spectacle.

Patients in the DPC model are not subjected to this shared space of unease; instead, they are promptly seen upon arrival with little to no time spent in the waiting room, preserving their health and safeguarding others from potential exposures.

Bonus Features of DPC

One standout feature of the DPC model is its ability to offer lab tests at significantly lower prices. This affordability is achieved because the majority of DPC practices negotiate directly with lab vendors to secure wholesale pricing, leveraging the combined volume of their patient bases to obtain prices well below what's typically charged at retail. Clinics then take this benefit and extend it directly to their patients. This negotiating savvy, coupled with a firm commitment to pricing transparency, ensures that patients fully understand their expenses outright, sidestepping the steep fees often encountered in traditional healthcare environments.

The streamlined nature of the DPC model also cuts down on administrative overhead, reducing costs that translates into more savings for patients. Oftentimes, the monthly membership fee that is a hallmark of the Direct Primary Care model covers basic lab tests, with the option for additional tests at significantly reduced prices. This makes medical care more attainable and budget-friendly, particularly for those without insurance. And for insured patients, DPC practices provide a more economical option for routine tests, enriching the outpatient experience by merging value with high quality care.

Another exciting feature of some DPC practices is the ability for their doctors to dispense medications directly to patients. This means you can often leave your doctor's office with your prescribed medications in hand, skipping that stressful trip to the pharmacy and reducing out-of-pocket medication costs. DPC physicians typically acquire generic medications at significantly lower prices than that of retail and pass these savings directly to their patients. While not every DPC clinic offers this service, those that do provide a substantial convenience and an even more substantial amount of savings.

I often see patients' eyes widen in surprise when they learn just how inexpensive their medications can be when they get them through our clinic. For instance, many are shocked to discover that a chronic medication like amlodipine, which typically costs around $4.50 for a 30-day supply at the pharmacy, is just $3.78 for a 90-day supply through our clinic. And this is the price without any coupons or special sales. This medication option not only simplifies the process of managing conditions like high blood pressure or high cholesterol; it also makes treatment far more reachable and cost-effective. It's another dynamic way DPC practices are redefining patient-centered care, ensuring you have more affordability and transparency in your healthcare journey.

Looking Back

So, it should be evident that Direct Primary Care reshapes the healthcare system with its patient-first philosophy, blending of personal care with straightforward pricing, and direct access to doctors when and where needed. Each DPC clinic shares a commitment to putting patients first and this approach allows you the freedom to choose your doctor based on personal fit, not insurance constraints.

Direct Primary Care is about ensuring you receive attentive, tailored care on your schedule, fostering meaningful interactions with your doctor, whether it's through extended face-to-face and virtual visits or convenient communication via phone or email at extended hours. By sidestepping the unpredictable bills and bureaucratic tangles of insurance-driven care, DPC makes medical costs clear and manageable, where same-day appointments, negligible wait times, and the elimination of financial surprises enhances your experience.

In essence, Direct Primary Care presents a compelling case for reevaluating our healthcare priorities. By offering a model that champions accessibility, efficiency, and transparency, DPC not only challenges the status quo but also sets a new standard for patient-centered care.

Chapter 5
The Amazing Benefits of
Direct Primary Care for Businesses

Imagine a healthcare system where employees can see their doctor whenever they need to, without the usual headaches of long waits, confusing bills, or endless insurance paperwork. Sounds too good to be true? Well, this is exactly what Direct Primary Care offers, and it's transforming how businesses handle their healthcare needs. Let's chat about how DPC can boost a company's bottom line while keeping its employees healthy and happy.

When your team is healthy, everyone wins. DPC gives employees direct access to their doctors without the hassles of traditional healthcare. Picture this: an employee wakes up feeling under the weather. Instead of waiting weeks for an appointment or wasting hours in a crowded waiting room, they can see their doctor that same day! This immediate access means health problems are addressed before they spiral, leading to fewer sick days and having a workforce that's always ready to tackle their tasks.

Another important fact we all know – healthy employees are productive employees. Since health issues are managed quickly with DPC, it reduces the time employees spend away from work. A fancier way of saying this is Direct Primary Care decreases absenteeism among employees. Think about it: fewer employees being out because of illness equals more focus on the job and less downtime for the business. Employees who aren't bogged down by health worries are usually more engaged and motivated, which naturally leads to better performance and a positive work environment.

Now, let's talk about the thing most businesses have to always consider to remain viable – *money*. DPC can assist with businesses having more of this by significantly cutting down on its healthcare costs. Instead of the unpredictable expenses that come with traditional insurance, DPC offers a flat monthly fee for each employee. This covers all of their primary care needs without co-pays or surprise bills. Imagine being able to budget your healthcare overhead without the fear of unexpected spikes. Plus, with fewer emergency room visits and specialist referrals, your overall medical expenditures drop. And since DPC manages most primary care needs, your insurance premiums can also go down as you shift toward plans that cover only major medical events.

Let's move on to the fact that managing traditional health plans can feel like navigating a maze. Well with Direct Primary Care, the path is much clearer. There's less paperwork, fewer claims to process, and uncomplicated billing, allowing your human resources team to focus on more strategic tasks instead of getting bogged down in a landslide of medical admin. Many DPC doctors work with employers of varying sizes to simplify the implementation of DPC plans. Their flexible schedules mean they can meet with HR, business owners, and employees at their places of business to discuss the DPC model and the services they offer, making it easier to adopt this inventive strategy.

Those special doctors will also do things like create customized membership plans that include additional services like basic labs for a single fee. Just in case you're wondering how to split the costs, many DPC practices will allow employers to cover the DPC fees entirely or share them with employees. Either way, it's a win for both sides. And some DPC doctors may even serve as the on-site physician for a given day of the week providing medical services directly to employees at the job.

Another positive consideration for Direct Primary Care in today's competitive job market is how offering something like this unique model can set you apart. DPC is a standout benefit that not only attracts top talent but also keeps your current employees happy. Prospective employees will see DPC as a hassle-free, economical healthcare option, making your job offers even more attractive. And for your existing team, knowing their healthcare is simple and effective boosts loyalty and job satisfaction, which translates into lower turnover and less money spent on hiring and training new staff.

A compelling example of how the DPC system has worked well for an employer would be a growing manufacturing company who implemented the model and achieved a 46% reduction in per-employee-per-year healthcare costs. Over the first four years, they experienced a 42% reduction in primary care claims and a 30% reduction in specialist care claims. This substantial cost saving is a testament to the efficiency and effectiveness of the DPC model. By providing comprehensive and preventive care on-site, the company not only lowered its healthcare expenses but also saw a significant boost in employee wellness and engagement.

Direct Primary Care offers a host of benefits that can transform your approach to employee healthcare. From healthier, more productive employees to significant cost savings and simplified management, DPC can make a real difference for your business. As you think about the future of your company's healthcare strategy, consider how DPC can help you build a healthier, happier, and more efficient workforce.

Having established the core tenets of Direct Primary Care, we're now set to navigate the terrain often occupied by DPC skeptics. In the next chapter, we will venture into this territory, dedicating time to dispel the myths, address concerns, and explore comparisons with concierge medicine, further clarifying the distinctive benefits and realities of DPC.

Chapter 6
Debunking Myths, Addressing Concerns, and Comparing DPC to Concierge Medicine

So we know that within the maze of modern healthcare, complexity and delusions often overshadow the true essence of care. We also know Direct Primary Care consistently emerges as a much clearer and simpler alternative. However, as its popularity grows, a fog of myths and misconceptions tends to obscure its real benefits. This confusion is further compounded when comparing DPC to concierge medicine, a similar yet distinctly different model. Armed with a mission to shed light on the matter, let's set out to demystify these topics.

Myth #1:

Direct Primary Care

is only for the wealthy.

Once upon a time, a narrative unfolded that Direct Primary Care was a privilege only the wealthy could afford – a sort of VIP ticket to the front of the healthcare line. We are not quite sure where this story first originated, but let the truth reveal that DPC is far from an exclusive club with a velvet rope at the entrance.

We previously mentioned that for an affordable monthly DPC membership, you gain enhanced access to primary care services. This inexpensive membership fee remains the same for those who have insurance and even those who do not. Some Direct Primary Care practices even offer memberships as little as $50 per month for adults, $25 per month for children, and even $1 per month for their beloved senior patients of a certain age. Talk about a budget-friendly show stopper.

Most importantly, this model also gives its patients this pricing outright, thereby discarding the fear of unexpected bills and heralding a much better tale of transparency and affordability.

The misconception that DPC is an elitist affair couldn't be further from the truth. DPC extends an invitation to all, offering a comprehensive healthcare experience that aligns with the average budget, proving that quality care doesn't have to come with a luxury price tag.

Myth #2:

Direct Primary Care just covers acute issues or chronic issues, but it doesn't do both.

You might've heard this rumor that Direct Primary Care doesn't quite cover all your health needs. There's a bit of a tug-of-war in opinions – some folks claim it's best for those ongoing, chronic conditions, while others swear it's your go-to for those sudden, acute issues. Well let's set the record straight about this once and for all. Imagine DPC as the ultimate versatile medical model, kind of like that trusty Swiss Army knife in your drawer that's ready for just about anything. Let's review some real-life moments where DPC shines.

Picture this, you're managing diabetes or high blood pressure – conditions that are long term and don't take a day off. In a DPC setting, your physician isn't just a distant figure behind a desk or a fleeting presence in a rushed appointment. They are there to guide you through all of the ups and downs, lab checks, and medication adjustments that come with each chronic ailment, tweaking the game plan as you go when needed so these diagnoses remain under control. It's custom, attentive care that adjusts as your needs do. Better yet, DPC manages your chronic conditions with the same precision as when you flip out the delicate tweezers and magnifying glass on that Swiss Army knife of yours.

Then there are those unexpected moments life throws at you. Say you're doing some DIY at home and *oops* – a nasty cut. Instead of spending hours in an ER waiting room, your DPC doc can stitch you up right there in their office. And it doesn't stop there. Woke up feeling like you got hit by a truck and suspect it's the flu? Or maybe it's that pesky bladder infection again, or a sore throat that feels like swallowing sandpaper? Your DPC practice is equipped to handle these urgent needs too, often with in-house testing for a quick diagnosis. No more bouncing around from place to place. So, you might say that DPC handles your acute issues with the same readiness and efficiency as when you snap out the knife and scissors on your trusty Swiss Army knife.

Let's also shine a light on the preventive tools at DPC's disposal. You should know that Direct Primary Care goes beyond merely reacting to health issues – it's fundamentally about proactive strategies designed to keep you in peak condition. This includes regular health screenings that catch potential issues before they become problems, coupled with personalized health coaching to guide your daily wellness choices. By focusing on preventive care, DPC ensures that you're not just treated for the conditions you have today, but also shielded from those you might face tomorrow. Consider DPC akin to the screwdriver, corkscrew, and fingernail file on your Swiss Army knife – an essential tool not just for repairs but for maintaining your health, ready to prevent problems before they even start.

Now imagine you're managing a busy life with sudden allergy attacks alongside a chronic condition like diabetes. In a traditional healthcare setting, you might end up bouncing between specialists or waiting days or weeks for an appointment. With DPC, you can get immediate care for your allergy flares today, a comprehensive diabetes check-up tomorrow, and an in-depth nutritional assessment next week to proactively manage your blood sugar and blood pressure levels. All of this is overseen by a physician who knows your health history intimately and tailors both preventive and immediate care to your unique needs. And perhaps the best part of this setup is that your price doesn't vary by the level of medical complexity and it doesn't increase with each clinic visit.

What it all boils down to is this: DPC isn't about limiting your care; it's about expanding it in a way that's genuinely focused on you. Whether it's about prevention, chronic illness management, or dealing with life's little emergencies, your DPC doctor is there to navigate it all with you, offering a blend of care that's as comprehensive as it is compassionate. It's healthcare that's not just about treating you when you're sick (aka, the traditional model), but also about helping you live your best life every day.

Myth #3:

You can't use health insurance at all if you are in a DPC practice.

There's a common misunderstanding that you can't use insurance at all with Direct Primary Care. Let's clear this up, shall we? While most DPC fees are generally paid out of pocket, this does not stop you from using your insurance for other medical needs. For instance, when your DPC doctor prescribes medications, you can use your insurance at the pharmacy just like you normally would. Similarly, if you need lab work, you have the option to process these through your insurance if that's your preference. Furthermore, insurance is perfectly applicable for services outside the DPC scope, such as specialist visits, imaging, or hospitalizations. Many patients also leverage their Health Savings Accounts (HSAs) or Flexible Spending Accounts (FSAs) to cover their DPC fees, though regulatory acceptance may vary pending your location or employer's specifications.

I often say to our prospective patients, in Direct Primary Care, our plan is to use insurance responsibly and not for every little thing that comes up. So we don't hassle with insurance for things like co-pays, deductibles, or premiums, but try to only use it for medications, imaging, labs, and referrals when absolutely necessary. In this way, DPC provides an added layer of unique care by complementing, rather than replacing, your insurance benefits.

Myth #4:

There's no coverage for hospital visits or specialists with Direct Primary Care.

Here's a myth that frequently causes unnecessary worry: the idea that with Direct Primary Care, you're left uncovered for hospital visits or consultations with specialists. While it's true that Direct Primary Care specifically focuses on primary care, DPC practices far and wide play a key role in coordinating your care with hospitals and specialists whenever that's needed. What's equally important is that many patients smartly pair their DPC membership with a high-deductible insurance plan, where possible, or a health sharing plan. Now I know what most of you are thinking, *What's a health sharing plan?* Well, allow a DPC doctor to explain this a bit more.

A health sharing plan is an alternative to traditional health insurance where its members, often sharing common ethical or religious beliefs, pool their money to help cover each other's medical expenses. Unlike conventional insurance, these plans are not bound by the same regulations, which can provide more flexibility in terms of coverage and pricing structure. Within these plans, members contribute a set monthly amount, which is then distributed to cover the medical bills of those in need within the community. This approach not only fosters a sense of shared responsibility but can also be more cost-effective, making it an attractive option for many who seek a more community-oriented way to manage healthcare expenses.

Nearly all DPC doctors are well-versed in health sharing plans while virtually all traditional primary care doctors have no clue they exist. That's another point on the scoreboard for DPC! I take great pride in being possibly the first DPC doctor to introduce this concept to you, just as I do when I introduce this to my very own patients for the first time who routinely find traditional insurance options unaffordable or unavailable to them.

Believe it or not, the same day I wrote this section of the book, I had this very conversation about health sharing plans with an elderly patient of mine and her daughter. This sweet lady had recently migrated to the United States and she was told that she would have to wait five years to qualify for health insurance coverage. It goes without saying that my patient's daughter was not only worried about her mother's health, but also how she would deal with the huge medical bills that would follow if her mother went to a hospital or specialist. I'm glad to say that by integrating DPC with a health sharing plan, they now have peace of mind knowing they're covered for everything from regular check-ups to unexpected medical needs and referrals. This combination ensures that they – and you – are well-equipped to handle any health scenario with confidence and security.

Myth #5:

Direct Primary Care

is a new, untested model.

You might have heard some skepticism about Direct Primary Care being a shiny new toy in the world of healthcare – therefore it's thought to be untested and unproven. Let's dispel that notion right away. DPC has been in practice since the late-1990s, with the first official DPC practice being founded in 1997. This model has since grown, especially in the mid-2000s, as more physicians sought alternatives to the constraints of traditional fee-for-service systems dominated by insurance billing and complex regulations. The movement has more recently begun to capture broader attention.

As of 2024, there are approximately 2,294 DPC practices operating across forty-eight states and Washington, D.C. As of 2021, the DPC model has seen an average annual growth rate of 36%, with total growth reaching 241% from 2017 to 2021. This substantial growth reflects the model's increasing popularity among physicians and patients seeking alternatives to traditional insurance-based care. Across the country, established DPC practices have been demonstrating their value for years and decades alike, achieving successful outcomes and high patient satisfaction. Patients of DPC enjoy more personal time with their doctors, shorter waits, and often superior health management, showing that DPC is not just an experiment, but a proven and highly sustainable model.

Myth #6:

Doctors going into the DPC model are causing a shortage of physicians in primary care.

There's a persistent myth that doctors moving into Direct Primary Care are causing a shortage of primary care physicians. But let's truly investigate this myth and provide some factual insights which should easily demonstrate how inaccurate this statement truly is.

We actually spent time on this very topic during one of our Byja Radio podcast episodes. During the episode, my co-host George – who happens to be our very first patient at Byja Clinic – and I shed light on several crucial factors contributing to these shortages. First, many physicians face burnout and job dissatisfaction due to overwhelming administrative tasks and high patient volumes, leaving them unable to deliver the quality care they aspire to provide. The COVID-19 pandemic only amplified these stresses, leading some healthcare workers to leave the field entirely. Additionally, an aging workforce means many primary care doctors are retiring, with insufficient new physicians being trained to fill their shoes. Geographical imbalances exacerbate this issue further, as rural and underserved areas struggle to attract and retain physicians due to less attractive compensation and working conditions compared to urban settings.

Moreover, financial and educational barriers play a significant role. The high cost of medical education and the debt that follows can deter many from entering the field, while the long years of training required can be a further disincentive. Shifts in career preferences are also evident, with newer generations favoring professions that offer a better work-life balance, less-demanding education requirements, or more immediate financial rewards. Lastly, moral injury – the topic we previously covered in Chapter 2 – only further contributes to the physician exodus from the traditional primary care system.

So, contrary to the myth that DPC exacerbates physician shortages, this model actually provides several effective solutions to the very issues that are driving doctors away from primary care. For starters, DPC significantly reduces the administrative burden that plagues traditional practice. Imagine physicians practicing in a healthcare environment where they don't have to wrestle with insurance paperwork or spend endless hours on billing. By eliminating these administrative hassles, DPC allows doctors to dedicate more of their time and energy to patient care. This not only lightens their workload but also rekindles their passion for medicine, making their professional lives far more satisfying.

Moreover, DPC offers a much better work-life balance. We know that traditional practices often saddle doctors with large patient panels and demanding schedules. In contrast, Direct Primary Care practices typically manage smaller

Byja Blueprint

patient panels, so doctors get to spend a far more meaningful amount of time with each patient. The freedom to truly get to know patients and attend to their needs in a relaxed, unrushed manner is revolutionary for many physicians, leading to greater job satisfaction and less burnout. It should come as no surprise that this reduction in patient volume leads to less time trapped in the office and more time to enjoy life outside of work.

The benefits of DPC extend beyond just time management; it also enhances patient relationships. With fewer patients, DPC doctors will build deeper, more personal connections with those they treat. Longer visits and the ability to focus on each individual's unique health journey also means that DPC doctors get to offer more comprehensive and compassionate care. This personalized approach is not only more satisfying for physicians but also for patients, who openly appreciate the attentive and thorough care they receive.

Financial stability and independence are two additional advantages of DPC. While traditional models often tie physician income to patient volume and complex billing systems, DPC operates on a straightforward monthly fee. This model can provide a predictable and steady income, which allows doctors to focus on their practice without the financial anxiety that comes from fluctuating revenues and insurance dependencies that can change in the blink of an eye at practically any given moment. By simplifying fiscal matters, DPC lets its doctors take control of their finances, fostering a more balanced and fruitful career.

DPC also places a strong emphasis on preventive care, shifting the focus from treating illnesses to preventing them. This proactive approach leads to better overall health outcomes for patients and a more rewarding professional experience for doctors. Fewer emergency interventions and acute crises mean doctors can concentrate on maintaining and improving their patients' health, rather than constantly putting out fires.

Finally, Direct Primary Care is particularly appealing to newly minted physicians. Medical students and residents often look at the traditional healthcare landscape and see a future filled with burnout and red tape. DPC offers a refreshing alternative – a career path that promises meaningful patient interactions, reduced administrative burdens, and a better quality of life. By presenting a more inviting and sustainable option, DPC has the potential to attract a new generation of physicians into primary care, helping to mitigate the very shortages it's accused of causing.

Myth #7:

DPC is Just Another Version of Concierge Medicine.

The common misconception that Direct Primary Care is just another version of concierge medicine is the final myth we will address. Let me just say that while they might seem similar at a glance, DPC and concierge medicine have some fundamental differences. Cost differences are a significant distinction between these two approaches. Concierge medicine typically comes with a higher price tag for its memberships and more often than not it uses add-on services and packages that go beyond primary care. These add-ons come in many different formats and might include non-standard lab panels, wellness programs, meal plans, shopping lists, exclusive access to specialists, and/or luxury amenities. It shouldn't be a shocker that as more things are added on, the pricier this concierge model becomes. In contrast, DPC tends to focus solely on primary care and does this at a lower, more predictable cost, making it available to a broader range of patients. It's designed to be budget-friendly, often costing less than your monthly cell phone bill, while still providing high-quality, individualized care without the extra frills.

Insurance billing is another area where these models boldly diverge. Concierge practices often bill their patients' insurance plans for both primary care and other medical services in addition to directly charging those same patients for memberships and add-on services, adding layers of complexity to healthcare costs and administration. This can easily lead to confusion and higher overall costs for patients. On the other hand, Direct Primary Care purposefully simplifies the process by eliminating insurance billing altogether for its services. In the DPC model, patients pay a simple monthly fee directly to their doctor, which covers their primary care needs, and avoids insurance in every way possible. This approach cuts out the middleman and avoids the double-billing conundrum patients often experience within concierge practices, thereby making the entire healthcare experience more candid and manageable.

Finally, consider that many concierge practices often require patients to commit to a year-long or months-long contract in advance, which can be a barrier to entry for those who prefer more flexibility. In contrast, DPC practices often offer month-to-month agreements, allowing patients to adapt their clinical arrangements as their needs change without long-term commitments. This flexibility is a huge plus for patients who value the freedom to choose how and when they receive care. While both Direct Primary Care and concierge medicine aim to improve the quality of care delivered and the overall patient experience, DPC achieves these aims by focusing on affordability, transparency, and flexibility, making it a distinct and inclusive option for many individuals and families.

It should be quite evident by now that Direct Primary Care offers a better, refreshing alternative to traditional and concierge medicine. By delivering high-quality care through affordability, simplicity, and deepened doctor-patient relationships and by debunking prevalent myths around the model, we've shown how DPC redefines primary care, making it more accessible and satisfying for both physicians and patients. We will now transition to Chapter 7, spotlighting real-life stories and revealing the profound impact Direct Primary Care has on patients and doctors alike. These accounts will underscore the genuine value and transformative power of the DPC model, bringing the theoretical benefits we've discussed to life through personal experiences.

Chapter 7
Real Stories of
DPC Patients and Doctors

In this chapter, the profound power of Direct Primary Care comes alive through compelling stories of both patients and DPC physicians. There are so many narratives I could share about our patients and the DPC doctors making an impact, but I chose these particular stories because they are exceptional in their outcomes and they have deeply inspired me on my DPC journey.

The doctors mentioned exemplify the versatility and depth of Direct Primary Care, spanning across diverse geographical areas and practice setups, while thriving in various focuses and settings. You'll also hear about patients who found renewed health and peace of mind through the personable care DPC provides. These stories illustrate the tangible benefits of Direct

Primary Care, demonstrating how this model not only enhances medical care but also enriches the doctor-patient relationship, fostering a more fulfilling healthcare journey for everyone involved.

Dr. Bliss

Dr. Garrison Bliss, a trailblazer in Direct Primary Care, transformed his approach to medicine after recognizing the limitations of traditional insurance-driven models. Dr. Bliss began his career in internal medicine and soon found himself dealing with the frustration of how insurance companies dictated care and drove up costs. This led him to establish Seattle Medical Associates in 1997, the first Direct Primary Care practice in the United States. This new model, which replaced insurance payments with a straightforward monthly fee, was born from a desire to make and keep medical care highly ethical. Within this good faith effort, patients would have direct access to their doctors, fostering a more personal and proactive healthcare approach.

Despite challenges, Dr. Bliss's breakthrough demonstrated how removing insurance intermediaries could enhance patient care and reduce costs. By offering forthright pricing and accommodating patients who couldn't afford the full fee, Dr. Bliss showed that DPC could be inclusive and effective. His work not only influenced numerous DPC practices nationwide, but also evolved into something that became self-sustaining, where DPC principles are now integrated throughout larger health systems.

In retirement, Dr. Bliss continues to advocate for Direct Primary Care, mentoring new practitioners and engaging in policy discussions to expand the model's reach. His vision remains centered on making high-quality, patient-focused primary care within reach for everyone, regardless of financial circumstances. Dr. Bliss's legacy in DPC demonstrates how a patient-centric model can provide sustainable care that is exceptional and reshape the medical landscape for the better.

Teresa and Her Sutures

Teresa is a self-employed cleaner who tirelessly works servicing houses and restaurants. Having no insurance, Teresa decided to join Byja Clinic so she would have access to cost-effective primary care. One day while cleaning a knife in a restaurant kitchen, she accidentally sustained a severe cut on her right hand. The laceration was bleeding heavily, and under normal circumstances, she would have headed straight to the emergency department (ED), facing a hefty bill. Instead, Teresa came to us and we treated her immediately on the same day. We managed to stop the bleeding and sutured the laceration without any wait or surprise costs.

But Teresa's ordeal didn't end there. As she continued working, her laceration reopened not once, not twice, but three more times over the next two weeks. Each time she returned to us, apologetic and worried. Nevertheless, we provided prompt care, closing her wound again and again and again without any delay or additional charges.

Now, had Teresa gone to the ED each time, she would have faced not only long wait times but also exorbitant costs. ED visits for lacerations can run into hundreds or even thousands of dollars, particularly when repeated visits are required. By utilizing our DPC services, Teresa saved significant time, avoided the stress of large unexpected bills, and received consistent, compassionate care. Her story underscores how DPC can be a lifeline for those without insurance, offering timely, inexpensive, and ongoing care without the financial and logistical burdens typically associated with emergency medical treatment.

Dr. Haynes

Dr. Delicia Haynes embodies the remarkable strength of Direct Primary Care, intertwining her personal journey with her professional mission to revolutionize how clinical care is delivered. As the CEO and founder of Family First Health Center in Daytona Beach, Florida, Dr. Haynes has dedicated her practice to a holistic, patient-centered approach, using the DPC model to help her patients thrive from the inside out.

Her path to DPC began in the early 2000s, when she started her career as a fee-for-service physician. She was driven by a vision to create the ideal medical environment based on her personal experiences as a patient. However, despite her efforts to deliver this type of care, the constraints of insurance-driven medicine soon took their toll. The endless paperwork, the limited time with patients, and the growing administrative burdens became overwhelming. By 2014, Dr. Haynes knew something had to change.

The turning point came when a significant cut in insurance reimbursements coincided with the loss of her biller to a local hospital system.

Facing a pivotal moment, she attended the National Primary Care Summit, where she discovered Direct Primary Care – a model that offered the promise of aligning clinical practices with her values.

Transitioning to DPC was not a magic cure for Dr. Haynes's struggles with depression, which she had battled since her high school years. However, it did provide the framework for her to regain control over her practice and her life.

With Direct Primary Care, Dr. Haynes could finally practice medicine as she had always intended – focusing on the patient, building meaningful relationships, and promoting true wellness without the interference of insurance companies. After changing to the DPC model, Dr. Haynes was able to complete her first book, *The Dawn,* which shines a light for physicians and medical students on ways of overcoming stress and depression.

One of the most poignant examples of how Direct Primary Care changed Dr. Haynes's life was her experience caring for her mother. In 2017, Dr. Haynes's mother was diagnosed with advanced uterine cancer. The flexibility of DPC allowed Dr. Haynes to be by her mother's side throughout her treatment, traveling frequently between Florida and Kentucky. Even during this emotionally taxing period, Dr. Haynes continued to manage her practice and provide care for her patients, thanks to the steady, predictable income of the DPC model and the amazing support of her medical team.

Xavier, David, and Their Employees

Let's explore the story of Xavier and David, local business owners operating a medical equipment company. Like many employers, they were frustrated with the quality of care and limited access their employees received under their standard health insurance plan. After hearing promising feedback about Direct Primary Care, they decided to enroll their team at Byja Clinic and cover the monthly DPC membership costs for their staff.

Their decision paid off quickly when an employee showed up to work with a severe headache and dangerously high blood pressure of 186/122. Xavier and David urged the employee to seek immediate evaluation with us. When we received their call for an appointment, they were delighted to find that we could see the employee the same day. He soon arrived at our office and was promptly evaluated, diagnosed, and prescribed medication, leaving with it in hand. That's right, it was all done without him needing an additional trip to the pharmacy. The efficiency and affordability of this care surprised the employee, who experienced relief from his headache within twenty-four hours thanks to our timely intervention.

Xavier and David were not only pleased with the swift, effective treatment but also relieved that their employee didn't have to miss several days of work – which would likely have been the case within the traditional healthcare setting requiring multiple trips to the doctor or emergency department. Encouraged by the positive outcomes, they began enrolling new employees and their own families in our DPC practice from that day forward.

They were also thrilled with the extended services we offer at Byja Clinic, like medication-assisted weight loss programs, ear and nose piercings, and IV fluid administration. They were blown away even more when they learned that we also offer medical marijuana approvals through our Byja MC Company business, all with upfront, transparent pricing.

With DPC, they've seen substantial improvements in their employees' health and well-being without the worry of surprise bills or lengthy disruptions in their team's work schedules. This experience reaffirmed their decision to choose Direct Primary Care, offering both superior care and operational efficiency for their business.

Dr. Flanagan

Dr. Clint Flanagan's journey to becoming a leading figure in Direct Primary Care is a tale of vision, determination, and a drive to improve healthcare. Raised in Nebraska, Dr. Flanagan was influenced early on by positive experiences with local primary care doctors and a stint in a high school Explorers Club focused on medicine. After completing medical school and a residency in family medicine, he worked in both rural and emergency medicine settings, including service in Iraq as part of the Army Medical Corps.

His passion for patient-centered care and frustration with the fee-for-service model led him to found Nextera Healthcare in 2009, Colorado's first Direct Primary Care program. Nextera's innovative model offers patients unlimited access to care for a monthly fee, fostering better doctor-patient relationships without the bureaucratic burden of insurance-based systems.

Under Dr. Flanagan's leadership, Nextera Healthcare has grown exponentially, now operating over 150 clinics across twenty states and serving a diverse range of patients, including individuals and employees from various industries. The model, initially termed "monthly membership medicine," evolved into what is now recognized as Direct Primary Care, focusing on providing comprehensive primary care without the hassles of traditional insurance.

Dr. Flanagan's commitment to this model is reflected in Nextera's success and its recognition as one of the most promising healthcare companies. His influence extends beyond his practice through his involvement in shaping healthcare policy, contributing to Direct Primary Care legislation in multiple states, and advocating for the model at national forums. By emphasizing the value of the doctor-patient relationship and innovative care delivery, Dr. Flanagan exemplifies the groundbreaking potential of DPC in modern healthcare.

Mary, Adam, and The Diaper Rash

Mary and Adam have been members of Byja Clinic for several years, but their journey with us began under challenging circumstances. Despite her best efforts, Mary couldn't secure insurance through her employer or the marketplace. As a result, she found herself without coverage while caring for two young children, including her sixteen-month-old son, Adam.

One Saturday morning, a distressed Mary called our office in a panic. Adam had developed a severe diaper rash that was rapidly spreading down his legs. Recognizing the urgency and hearing the worry in Mary's voice, we assured her that we would make time to see Adam despite the clinic being officially closed. Mary was deeply grateful for the immediate support and the personal touch we offered.

When Adam was brought in, we confirmed the severity of the rash. After cleaning the affected area, we applied a soothing cream and barrier ointment, providing Adam with instant relief. We also supplied Mary with prescription medication directly from our office at a fraction of the cost she would have faced at a pharmacy. Over the next few days, Mary was able to share photos of Adam's recovery with us via text messaging, confirming the rash was healing well.

This timely and compassionate care not only resolved Adam's health issue but also reinforced Mary's trust in the DPC model. Today, their family remains a devoted part of our practice, appreciating the continuous, attentive care we provide.

Dr. Norris

Dr. Jade Norris (aka Dr. Jade) has redefined what personalized clinical care means for her community in Las Vegas. Known for her commitment to excellence in care and her dedication to improving the physician work-life balance, Dr. Jade's story is one of inspiration and creativity.

Dr. Jade discovered Direct Primary Care during her second year of residency training. It was a casual conversation with one of her attending physicians that would set her on a new path. When asked about her future plans, Dr. Jade shared her desire to become a community doctor, fostering deep relationships with her patients while also maintaining a healthy work-life balance. Her attending physician immediately suggested she look into DPC, a model Dr. Jade had never heard of before.

Intrigued, Dr. Jade dove into researching Direct Primary Care that very night. She joined online communities, attended virtual conferences, and connected with other DPC physicians. As she immersed herself in the world of DPC, Dr. Jade found that it aligned perfectly with her vision for practicing medicine – focusing on patient care without the burdens of insurance paperwork and administrative tasks.

Her DPC practice, NSPIRE Primary Care, opened its doors in Las Vegas immediately following her graduation from residency. Here, Dr. Jade enjoys the freedom to provide unhurried, tailored care, ensuring her patients receive the attention they deserve. Unlike traditional models where physicians are often overwhelmed by patient volume and administrative duties, Dr. Jade's approach emphasizes quality over quantity, allowing her to build genuine, long-lasting relationships with her patients.

Today, Dr. Jade uses the power of social media to help grow her DPC practice. Throughout her posts you can easily see her commitment to provide education to her followers on topics related to both health and Direct Primary Care. Her story is a testament to the pioneering potential of DPC, a place where doctors can create their very own unique practices even if they have just completed residency.

Simon and His Swollen Elbow

Simon is a skilled barber and proud Navy veteran, who always turned to the Veteran Affairs (VA) system for his medical needs. However, after enrolling with us at Byja Clinic, he truly discovered a new level of personal and budget-friendly care that has reshaped his health journey from that point forward.

Simon's story took a turn when he began experiencing intense elbow pain and swelling in his dominant arm – critical for his work. Despite his best efforts to rest and manage the pain, the swelling persisted, making his daily tasks increasingly challenging.

When Simon visited our clinic, we confirmed that his elbow had developed fluid accumulation due to a bursitis flare. We initially recommended conservative treatments: wrapping the elbow, applying ice, and taking prescription-strength medication. But after a week, while the pain slightly improved, the swelling remained stubbornly unchanged. Understanding Simon's need to use his hands for his livelihood, we decided to take a more direct approach: an in-office drainage and injection procedure.

In the clinic, Simon's elbow was carefully prepped and sterilized. Using a needle, we precisely drained the excess fluid from the swollen area, which provided immediate relief from the pressure and discomfort. After draining the fluid, we administered a corticosteroid injection directly into the elbow to reduce inflammation and promote healing. Simon, understandably apprehensive about the procedure, found it to be much less daunting than he had anticipated. The procedure was completed seamlessly, with minimal pain, thanks to a local anesthetic and appropriate technique.

As Simon sat up, relieved from the immediate discomfort, he hesitantly asked about the cost of the procedure. His eyes widened in disbelief when he learned it was only $12, and that was to cover the cost of the steroids. He was astounded by the affordability, which starkly contrasted with the high costs he had anticipated. Simon humorously remarked that he wished he had discovered DPC years ago.

To this day, Simon remains a dedicated patient, grateful for the efficient and affordable care that has allowed him to swiftly return to his craft of being a barber.

Dr. Lassey

Dr. Vance Lassey's journey into Direct Primary Care was sparked by growing frustrations with the traditional healthcare system. As a seasoned family physician in Holton, Kansas, he found himself mired in the complexities of insurance billing, endless paperwork, and a lack of genuine patient connection. Despite his passion for medicine, these bureaucratic hurdles left him feeling constrained and disillusioned. In 2016, driven by a desire to reclaim the essence of doctoring, he transitioned to the DPC model, founding Holton Direct Care. This shift allowed him to focus on what truly mattered: building meaningful relationships with his patients, free from the red tape of third-party payers.

In his DPC practice, Dr. Lassey discovered a renewed joy in medicine. The simplified financial structure, where patients pay a single monthly fee for direct access, enabled him to offer longer, more personal appointments, often with same-day availability. This model not only alleviated the administrative burden but also enhanced patient care, as he could now spend adequate time understanding their needs and providing them with his comprehensive, uninterrupted attention. His practice flourished, with many patients appreciating the transparency and accessibility of his care.

Additionally, Dr. Lassey's practice is unique because it operates in a very rural area and was among the first to demonstrate the potential for large-scale DPC growth in such settings. Dr. Lassey also offers a broad spectrum of services within Holton Direct Care, including his delivery of orthopedic care to his patients and regularly performing numerous outpatient surgical procedures where needed.

Through DPC, Dr. Lassey found a sustainable way to practice medicine that aligned with his values, revitalizing his career and strengthening his commitment to medicine overall.

Dr. Lassey's story underscores the life-changing capability of Direct Primary Care. By eliminating insurance intermediaries, he reclaimed autonomy over his practice, leading to both professional satisfaction and improved patient outcomes. His experience highlights how DPC can revive a physician's passion for medicine, fostering a clinical environment where doctors and patients thrive together.

Mark and His Hair Loss

Mark, a man deeply frustrated by his thinning hair, was on a long quest for a specific solution. While searching for reputable solutions, a friend had mentioned platelet-rich plasma (PRP) therapy, a promising but elusive solution for hair regrowth. Having explored various clinics, he was disheartened by the high costs and the fact that none accepted insurance for the treatment he was seeking. Driven by the hope of reversing his hair loss, Mark reached out to us at Byja Clinic to inquire if we offered PRP treatments.

To his relief, we not only provided PRP services but also did so at a significantly more affordable rate than the other clinics he had contacted. During his initial visit, we evaluated the areas of concern on his scalp and confirmed that PRP would be an effective treatment for his type of hair loss. Mark decided to proceed, scheduling a series of PRP sessions. The treatment involved drawing a small amount of his blood, processing it to concentrate the platelets, and injecting the platelet-rich plasma into his scalp. This non-surgical procedure stimulated his hair follicles, promoting natural hair growth.

Mark was astounded by the results. Within the first two weeks, he noticed new hair growth in the previously thinning areas. Over the subsequent PRP sessions, his hair continued to fill in, restoring not just his hairline but his confidence as well. The cost-effectiveness and professionalism of our services led Mark to enthusiastically refer several friends and family members to our clinic.

His experience underscores the significance of our commitment to providing accessible, effective treatments in a supportive environment – addressing issues that many men find difficult to discuss openly. Mark's journey with PRP is a true testament to the remarkable outcomes the DPC model offers to patients.

Dr. Purcell

Dr. Shane Purcell's transition to Direct Primary Care not only reinvigorated his practice but also positively altered the health of the employees of his county. After experiencing the limitations of traditional insurance-driven healthcare, Dr. Purcell embraced DPC to build a more meaningful relationship with his patients. By 2015, he had established the first Direct Primary Care clinic in Anderson County, South Carolina, alongside a colleague. Their model thrived on a simple monthly membership, allowing Dr. Purcell to focus on patient care rather than insurance bureaucracy.

In 2016, Dr. Purcell's innovative approach caught the attention of Anderson County officials who were searching for a more effective healthcare solution for their employees. However, it took over two years to convince the county to make the move to a direct plan. After initial meetings in 2016, it wasn't until 2019 that Dr. Purcell and his team began seeing county employees. This lengthy process was worth the wait, as the collaboration meant that county employees could access care that was exceptional and personal through Dr. Purcell's clinic, with the county covering the cost of labs, medications, and office visits. This arrangement significantly reduced health related expenses for the county while providing better care for their employees, who benefited from enhanced availability and more customized treatments based on each employee's needs.

Dr. Purcell's work with Anderson County exemplifies the power of Direct Primary Care in addressing the broader health needs of a community. His partnership with the municipality showcased how local governments could leverage the DPC model to offer their employees fiscally responsible and comprehensive healthcare, ultimately improving health outcomes and reducing costs. This collaboration not only solidified Dr. Purcell's commitment to Direct Primary Care but also demonstrated its viability as a scalable healthcare solution for municipalities and other large organizations.

As we conclude this chapter, we have witnessed firsthand the heartfelt stories of both patients and doctors within Direct Primary Care. These real-life experiences highlight the profound ways DPC fosters amazing care while delivering even more amazing outcomes, enabling patients to regain their health and peace of mind while allowing physicians to rediscover the joy in their practices.

In our next chapter, we turn our attention to some of the different approaches and unique focuses within the Direct Primary Care landscape. We will explore the diverse models DPC practices develop and employ, from specialized services to innovative operational strategies, shedding light on how this flexible model can be tailored to meet the specific needs of various communities and patient populations.

Chapter 8
Diverse Models and Unique Focuses within Direct Primary Care

We will now shift our focus to the various ways Direct Primary Care practices are designed and implemented across different settings. This chapter will uncover the breadth of approaches that make DPC a versatile and adaptable solution in healthcare. From outpatient primary care to niche specialties, direct care proves its capacity to cater to a wide range of patient needs. By examining these diverse models and unique focuses, we will see how Direct Primary Care not only enhances patient care but also empowers physicians to tailor their practices in novel and meaningful ways.

Home Visits

Imagine your doctor coming to your place of residence for a check-up, just like in the good old days. That's precisely what DPC home visits bring back – a much-needed personal and convenient touch to healthcare. This service is indispensable for many, especially the elderly, those with chronic illnesses and special needs, or anyone who finds it tough to make it to a clinic. Instead of wrestling with traffic, waiting rooms, and tight schedules, your medical care comes to you. Your doctor sees you in your own space, getting a true sense of your lifestyle and environment, which helps in crafting a more tailored health plan. It's not solely about convenience; it's about creating a deeper, more meaningful doctor-patient relationship that traditional settings often miss.

For Direct Primary Care physicians, home visits offer a breath of fresh air compared to the relentless pace of traditional practice. By stepping out of the clinic and into the patient's home, doctors can escape the administrative grind and high patient volumes that typically define their workday. This shift allows them to reclaim their passion for medicine by spending meaningful, unhurried time with each patient, focusing on comprehensive care rather than just ticking boxes on a chart.

But the benefits go beyond just escaping the office. Home visits enable doctors to see patients in their own environments, providing distinctive insights into their daily lives that can't be gleaned from a sterile exam room. For instance, many pediatric DPC doctors have shared how home visits enable them to understand their patients in a more remarkable and holistic way. During a home visit, those doctors can observe a child's living environment, dietary habits, and even the family's routine – insights that are invaluable for crafting effective care plans. Imagine a pediatrician sitting on the living room floor, engaging with a child over their favorite toys, or a family doctor joining a family for a meal to better understand dietary concerns.

This level of observation enriches the doctors' understanding and helps tailor more effective treatment plans. Additionally, with fewer overhead costs like office space and staff, physicians can operate more flexibly and efficiently, allowing them to prioritize patient care over paperwork. Home visits in Direct Primary Care break down barriers and offer a blend of empathy and professional satisfaction that stands out in so many important ways.

Telehealth Only

Direct Primary Care practices that are telehealth only should easily transform how we think about medicine. Imagine getting all the benefits of a traditional doctor's visit while sitting in the bleachers during your child's soccer practice. Well, these telehealth only practices leverage the latest in telecommunication technology and sophisticated electronic health record systems to bring together patient engagement, effective treatment options, and convenience all into one user-friendly platform. It's having your doctor just a video call away. In these types of practices, DPC doctors may manage their practice remotely from Salt Lake City while their patients are in Washington, D.C., proving that telehealth can keep patients connected and cared for, no matter the distance.

What makes telehealth-only DPC really special is its flexibility and responsiveness to today's fast-paced, tech-savvy world. Patients love the instant access to their doctors without the hassle of traveling to a clinic, while cutting-edge communication apps and tools make it super easy to have quick chats with your doctor, schedule virtual check-ups, or even get advice through secure text messages. By operating exclusively online, these practices eliminate the hefty expenses associated with running a physical office – like rent, utilities, and maintenance costs. These newfound savings are then passed on to patients, so they can receive care that is economical and available to all without the traditional barriers.

Direct Specialty Care Models

Direct Specialty Care (DSC) is like the specialized sibling of Direct Primary Care. Both models revolutionize medical care by removing insurance hassles and building direct patient-doctor relationships. Just as DPC simplifies access to primary care, DSC streamlines your experience with specialists like hematologists, rheumatologists, or gynecologists. Imagine needing specialized care and simply paying a clear, upfront fee directly to the specialist. No insurance hoops, no surprise bills – just straightforward access to comprehensive evaluations, follow-ups, and ongoing management.

Like DPC, DSC allows you to build a direct, meaningful relationship with your doctor, ensuring that your healthcare is responsive to your needs. This model makes managing complex health issues much smoother and more predictable, offering a more engaging and efficient path to outstanding care.

Underserved Communities and Special Patient Populations

Some Direct Primary Care practices hold special value for underserved communities by providing even more inclusive, cost-effective, and individualized healthcare. In traditional models, these communities continually face barrier after barrier such as high costs, limited insurance coverage, geographic constraints, and the list goes on. DPC breaks down these barriers by offering openly distinct pricing and extremely flexible payment plans that all but eliminates the need for insurance.

In many instances, the Direct Primary Care model particularly benefits rural areas or economically disadvantaged neighborhoods where clinical options are sparse. For instance, many DPC clinics in rural communities will charge a very modest monthly fee of $50 per month for adult members, giving patients unlimited access to primary care services, including preventive care, chronic disease management, and urgent care for an economical rate. This direct payment model also allows Direct Primary Care practices to allocate more resources toward community outreach and support, tailoring medical services to meet the specific needs of the community. By eliminating the financial and administrative hurdles, DPC fosters an environment where everyone, regardless of income or insurance status, can receive quality care and build lasting bonds with their physicians.

Direct Primary Care also excels in meeting the unique needs of specific patient populations such as veterans, LGBTQ+ individuals, and elderly patients. These groups often require tailored approaches that traditional models might not adequately address. For veterans, DPC offers a continuous and personal healthcare experience that can complement or even enhance their existing VA benefits, providing easier access to both physical and mental health services without the wait times commonly seen in the VA system. For LGBTQ+ patients, Direct Primary Care practices regularly provide a safe, inclusive space where clinical care is not just about treating illnesses but also about understanding and supporting gender and sexual identity with sensitivity and respect. This individualized approach ensures that gender-affirming care, hormone replacement therapy, and other specific needs are addressed comprehensively and confidentially.

Elderly patients also benefit from the extended time and attention DPC physicians can offer, allowing for better management of chronic conditions, regular check-ups, and preventive measures that are often rushed or overlooked in traditional geriatric practices. By focusing on each individual's unparalleled health journey,

DPC creates a supportive environment where diverse patient populations receive respectful and effective care.

Pediatric Care

Pediatric DPC practices bring a fresh style to children's healthcare, making the experience more effective and less stressful for both kids and their families.

Traditional pediatric care often involves long wait times, brief appointments, and complicated insurance processes that can be especially challenging for young children and their parents. Pediatric DPC eliminates these hurdles by offering longer appointment times and same-day or next-day visits, ensuring that parents can address their concerns thoroughly and without rush.

This model allows pediatricians to focus on the whole child, from routine check-ups and vaccinations to developmental screenings and managing chronic conditions. The direct payment structure means parents know exactly what they're paying for, and with a simple, evident fee covering a wide range of services, families can avoid the unpredictability of insurance co-pays and deductibles. This approach fosters a strong, continuous relationship between the pediatrician and the family, which is crucial for understanding and responding to each child's unique health needs.

Pediatric Direct Primary Care stands out by supporting not only the physical health of children but also their developmental and emotional well-being within the context of family dynamics. The extended time pediatricians can spend with their young patients allows for a more thorough understanding of developmental milestones and early identification of issues such as behavioral or learning difficulties. Unlike traditional pediatric practices, pediatric DPC clinics offer longer, more attentive visits, allowing pediatricians to catch issues early and provide comprehensive care.

For instance, consider the case of a child who frequently misses school due to asthma flare-ups. In a traditional setup, their parents have to navigate insurance approvals and wait weeks for appointments with different specialists. Yet, at the pediatric DPC clinic, their doctor has the flexibility to see them quickly, adjust treatment plans on the spot, and provide parents with a direct line for ongoing support and management. This proactive approach not only stabilizes this condition but also significantly reduces school absences. Pediatric Direct Primary Care practices effectively minimize such disruptions by providing timely interventions, keeping children healthier, and ensuring they stay engaged in their education.

People Living with HIV

Direct Primary Care practices that specialize in treating people living with HIV often provide a distinctive and compassionate approach that addresses the multifaceted needs of these patients. Traditional healthcare models often involve fragmented care, where patients must juggle multiple appointments with various specialists, labs, and pharmacies, often leading to gaps in treatment and increased stress.

In contrast, DPC practices offer integrated care under one roof, streamlining this process with longer, unhurried appointments that foster a deeper understanding of each patient's medical history, medication lists including their various antiretroviral therapies, and personal circumstances.

Being that we specialize in this area of care at Byja Clinic, I can personally say that this model regularly allows us to provide our patients with comprehensive management of their HIV, including regular monitoring of their viral loads and CD4 counts, medication initiations and adjustments, and addressing co-existing conditions such as mental health issues and other areas that are impacted by their related social determinants of health.

For instance, at our Direct Primary Care clinic, we ensure our HIV+ patients can discuss any of their concerns about housing instability, employment issues, and family or relationship dynamics directly with their physicians in a supportive environment without the stigma that is routinely encountered in more traditional settings. We also make sure that our HIV patients get the latest and best antiretroviral medications and stay on top of their health screenings and vaccinations, which they often need more frequently than others.

Nonprofit DPC Models

Nonprofit Direct Primary Care practices provide a noble and compassionate healthcare model that prioritizes affordability and community impact. So, how do they make quality healthcare overtly accessible to those who usually would be left out? Well, nonprofit DPC clinics often do this through grants and donations, qualifying for special funding opportunities and partnerships, and reinvesting their earnings back into patient care and community services. This allows them to offer significantly lower membership fees and flexible payment options, catering especially to low-income families and uninsured individuals.

A creative example of this approach comes from St. Luke's Family Practice, a nonprofit Direct Primary Care organization in Modesto, California. In their nonprofit DPC clinic, funds from benefactors have been used to subsidize care for those who cannot afford it. Their model also allows uninsured patients to receive comprehensive care, including routine check-ups, chronic disease management, and preventive services without the stress of financial barriers. By eliminating the profit motive, these nonprofit DPC practices can focus on what truly matters: delivering even more tailored, superior care to everyone in the community.

Nonprofit DPC practices are also notable in their ability to engage and empower their communities. They often act as pillars of support, providing not just medical care but also education and resources to address broader social determinants of health.

At Byja Charitable Alliance, our nonprofit division of our Direct Primary Care practice, we provide access to an array of services that our patients need to address their physical, mental, and financial health. We have been successful in offering our patients, and our affiliate clinics' patients, services focused on nutrition education, financial planning and advising, and cognitive behavioral therapy. I am proud to say all of these services are offered to those patients at low costs that are communicated to them upfront without any surprises.

Other nonprofit Direct Primary Care organizations do things like partner with local food banks to assist patients facing food insecurity and offer free health screenings at community centers and health fairs.

Additionally, nonprofit DPC practices adapt quickly to meet emerging needs of their patients and communities as many practices provide telehealth services or home visits for these vulnerable patients. This flexibility and community-oriented approach create a supportive environment where patients feel valued and connected, leading to better health outcomes and a stronger, healthier community overall.

As we conclude our exploration of these diverse and distinctive approaches within the Direct Primary Care space, it's clear that innovation has made this model exceptionally adaptable to various patient needs and community contexts. From nonprofit DPC practices that reinvest in their communities to pediatric and HIV-focused DPC clinics that offer specialized, empathetic care, each model reflects a commitment to making healthcare unique, responsive, and open to all.

With such a variety of approaches available, the next step is finding a Direct Primary Care doctor who aligns with your specific needs and values.

In the upcoming chapter, we'll delve into practical advice and key considerations for choosing the right DPC doctor, ensuring you can benefit from a doctor who truly understands and supports you during your medical journey.

Chapter 9
Choosing the Right
DPC Doctor for You

So, you've decided that Direct Primary Care might be just what the doctor ordered for your healthcare needs. Great choice! But now you might be wondering: how do you find the perfect DPC doctor who fits your needs and lifestyle? In this chapter, we're going to make that process a breeze. We'll walk you through a few simple, practical tips to help you identify and choose a fantastic DPC doctor. Let's jump in and direct you to the perfect Direct Primary Care partner for your clinical quest.

If you're feeling a bit overwhelmed about finding the right Direct Primary Care doctor after an internet search had you clicking endlessly on website after website, but it left you coming up empty, you're not alone. Fortunately, the Mapper page on the website DPC Frontier is here to make your search much easier and more efficient. This handy tool lets you visually browse over 2,300 DPC practices across the U.S. Simply enter your ZIP code or zoom in on your town, and voila! You'll see a map dotted with Direct Primary Care practices near you.

Each listing gives you a quick snapshot of the practice, including their services and how to get in touch. Plus, you can see whether they are "Pure" DPC (meaning no insurance involved), "Hybrid" (a mix of DPC and traditional insurance), or "On-Site" (typically for company employees). This feature helps you find a practice that matches your insurance preferences and healthcare needs. With the DPC Mapper, you can easily explore and compare your options, making the process of choosing a DPC doctor simple.

There is another website that has a Member Directory that provides a fantastic resource for finding Direct Primary Care practices at your fingertips. This online tool is curated by the nonprofit DPC Alliance and is specifically tailored for anyone looking to find DPC practices across the United States. Whether you're a patient seeking a uniquely customized healthcare experience, an employer exploring health benefit options for your team, or a medical professional interested in the DPC model, this directory has something for you. You can search by location, physician name, or practice name, making it easy to find a doctor that matches your criteria. Each entry includes details about the practice, such as services offered, contact information, and even background information on the physicians. Moreover, the DPC Alliance ensures that the practices listed meet certain standards and principles of Direct Primary Care, adding a layer of trust to your search.

Another resource for finding Direct Primary Care practices are state-level DPC associations, which can be incredibly useful allies in this effort. These associations often maintain directories of local DPC practices, providing a more streamlined and robust view of your options compared to national lists. By tapping into their resources, you can find DPC doctors who not only meet high standards but also align with the specific healthcare environment of your state.

State-level Direct Primary Care associations also focus on advocating for the DPC model within their regions, ensuring that practices listed in their directories adhere to the principles of DPC and meet local regulatory requirements. This means you can trust that the practices they recommend are well-supported and compliant with state-specific laws, which can vary significantly across the country. Their directories often come with detailed information about each practice, including services offered, pricing models, and physician backgrounds, giving you a well-rounded view to make an informed choice.

Additionally, these associations provide insights into the local DPC landscape through networking events and community support, which can be invaluable. They might also feature testimonials or case studies from local patients and employers who have benefited from Direct Primary Care, helping you see real-world examples of how different practices operate. By connecting with a state-level DPC association, you're not just finding a doctor – you're gaining access to a wealth of local knowledge and a network of support that can guide you in your path to wellness.

If you're a physician navigating the Direct Primary Care landscape, conferences and seminars are invaluable for both newcomers and seasoned practitioners. These events offer a rich platform for learning, sharing experiences, and making meaningful connections within the DPC community. Educational sessions at these events provide deep dives into the nuts and bolts of running a Direct Primary Care practice, from start-up fundamentals to advanced operational strategies. Attendees can expect to gain insights into legal compliance, effective marketing techniques, and creative patient engagement methods.

These sessions are often led by experienced DPC practitioners and healthcare experts, making them a treasure trove of practical knowledge. Beyond learning, these events also offer networking opportunities to connect with peers, mentors, and industry leaders. Whether through formal sessions or informal gatherings, these connections can lead to valuable partnerships and collaborations.

Spending time at conferences like the DPC Summit and the Hint Summit, and regional events hosted by state DPC associations, can significantly enhance understanding of the Direct Primary Care model, provide actionable tools and knowledge, and help build a supportive network of like-minded professionals.

I must say that my initial experiences as an attendee at one of the national DPC conferences is what gave me the knowledge and the push to start my very own Direct Primary Care practice in 2020, despite being in a pandemic and having zero patients pre-enrolled with us. With me going from that type of beginning to now being a recurring speaker at those same conferences shows how things can change for the better in only a matter of years within Direct Primary Care. It should also confirm that these events are not just about learning – they're about building a community dedicated to the sensational care that DPC represents.

Social media networks can be surprisingly effective tools in your search to locate your Direct Primary Care practice of choice. LinkedIn can be your go-to for discovering DPC physicians through professional networks. By following Direct Primary Care practitioners and joining groups focused on DPC and primary care innovations, you can gain insights into various practices and connect directly with the clinicians. These connections might lead to recommendations or direct introductions to doctors who fit your healthcare needs.

On Facebook, you can also engage with community pages and groups dedicated to Direct Primary Care. Many DPC practices maintain active Facebook pages where they share health tips, updates, and patient testimonials. By following these pages and participating in discussions, you can get a feel for the practice's approach to care and patient engagement. Facebook's local groups can also be a treasure trove of recommendations and experiences from other patients who might have similar healthcare preferences.

Instagram provides a visual glimpse into the day-to-day operations of Direct Primary Care practices through photos and stories, which can help you assess the environment and culture of a potential practice. Lastly, YouTube is great for watching educational content and patient testimonials about DPC, offering a deeper understanding of what to expect from the care model and specific practices.

If you're hoping to increase your knowledge about Direct Primary Care, there's a stockpile of excellent podcasts out there to explore. *My DPC Story*, hosted by Dr. Maryal Concepcion, offers heartfelt stories from both DPC doctors and patients, giving you a personal glimpse into the day-to-day realities and benefits of the Direct Primary Care model.

For a broader perspective, *Exploring the Direct Primary Care Revolution* discusses how DPC is reshaping healthcare, featuring insights on cost savings and patient care improvements. *DPC News* keeps you up-to-date with the latest trends and developments in the Direct Primary Care world, covering everything from policy changes to practice management strategies.

And, of course, you should listen to *Byja Radio*, our very own podcast where George, aka Patient Zero, and I review practical tips, success stories, and the nuances of running a DPC practice. *Byja Radio* is designed to inspire and inform both prospective patients and practitioners about the profound potential of Direct Primary Care and it is a go-to source for understanding how DPC can provide more characteristic and efficient healthcare.

Finally, word-of-mouth referrals are perhaps the most effective method for finding the Direct Primary Care practice that best fits you and your needs. It should come as no surprise that recommendations from colleagues, co-workers, employers, family, and friends will provide trusted, first-hand insights into many things. Your family and friends could be a goldmine for recommendations as they may have direct experience with DPC practices or know someone who does. Also, keep in mind that word-of-mouth referrals from your co-workers or employer can be extremely useful if they have implemented or utilized Direct Primary Care services through workplace health plans.

On top of that, employers who offer DPC as part of their benefits package might also provide insights into practices known for excellent patient care and efficient service. These personal referrals often come with real life stories of how a particular practice or doctor has helped someone manage their health more effectively. By leveraging these stories and experiences, you can find a Direct Primary Care practice that not only meets professional standards but also provides a high level of patient satisfaction and personal care.

As you set out to find the ideal doctor for you, remember that it's about discovering a physician who truly resonates with your health needs and personal values. The selection process is not just about convenience – it's about establishing a meaningful partnership that will shape your future health. By choosing a great Direct Primary Care doctor who prioritizes your well-being and offers a tailor-made approach to healthcare just for you, it will ensure that your clinical experience is supportive, adaptive, and aligned with your goals. Take it from this DPC doctor that this decision marks the beginning of a collaborative doctor-patient relationship that will truly enhance your overall care for years or decades to come.

Conclusion

As we conclude this fantastic voyage of Direct Primary Care, it should be abundantly clear that this model offers a refreshing alternative to the challenges faced in traditional primary care. We thoroughly examined the shortcomings and pitfalls of the conventional healthcare system for both patients and physicians. Factors like limited time with doctors, excessive paperwork, and the overwhelming influence of insurance companies not only diminish the quality of care being delivered, they continually contribute to recurrent episodes of physician burnout and patient dissatisfaction.

Despite all of these dark spots in today's healthcare system, Direct Primary Care emerges as a solution that redefines the doctor-patient relationship, placing emphasis on accessibility, affordability, and personalized care. By removing the overly abundant constraints of insurance and focusing on what matters most – the delivery of high quality care – DPC allows for more meaningful interactions between doctors and patients. This model not only alleviates the administrative burdens on physicians, but also offers patients a direct line to their doctors, fostering more trust and improved patient outcomes.

For businesses, Direct Primary Care provides a fiscally responsible way to offer healthcare benefits to employees, reducing overall healthcare costs and increasing employee satisfaction and productivity. Myths surrounding DPC should be much more conspicuous at this point and the distinctions from concierge medicine further reinforce the availability and inclusivity of the Direct Primary Care model. Moreover, real life stories from patients and doctors in DPC practices repeatedly illustrate the transformative potential this model can have on both sides.

Lastly, the diversity of DPC practices, each with its unique focus, highlights the flexibility of Direct Primary Care and how these practices are free to cater to the different needs of the people they serve.

In essence, Direct Primary Care represents a shift from the business-as-usual style of medical care toward a more patient-centered and physician-friendly clinical model. It offers a glimpse into the future of primary care where the focus is truly on the patient, and physicians are empowered to deliver individualized care rather than focusing solely on the volume of patients that are seen each day.

As you consider your healthcare options or your strategy for providing healthcare benefits, I hope this book has gone BeYond Just Another Blueprint, guiding you toward Direct Primary Care as a viable and compelling choice. With DPC as your foundation, I have no doubt that you're poised for a more efficient, fulfilling healthcare journey, supported by a dedicated

Direct Primary Care community who remains committed to walking with you every step of the way.

So, what do you say?

Ready to join the DPC transformation?

www.ingramcontent.com/pod-product-compliance
Lightning Source LLC
Chambersburg PA
CBHW070405200326
41518CB00011B/2074